Let's Read!

 Read the Page

 Say It  Sound It  Spell It

 Game

 Repeat

 Stop

Why is wh yellow?

Yellow highlights represent letter teams that make a single sound or words with irregular decoding patterns.

Rose and Hope

Story by Suzanne Barchers
Illustrated by Meredith Johnson
Designed by Six Red Marbles

Rose and Hope woke up and put on robes. Rose and Hope are twins.

"Mom? Dad?" said Rose.
"Look, Rose," said
Hope. "There is a
note for us."

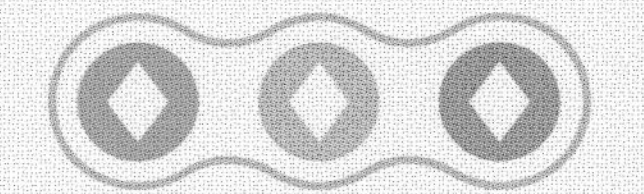

Dear Rose and Hope,
Let's begin your birthday game! Find us and we'll have a surprise for you!

Look for notes. Each note will have a new clue. Look under the lone cone for the next note.

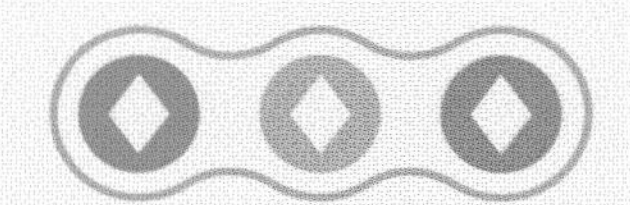

Rose and Hope look and look. They pick up the lone cone and find a note.

Hop to the cloves
next to the stove
for your next clue!

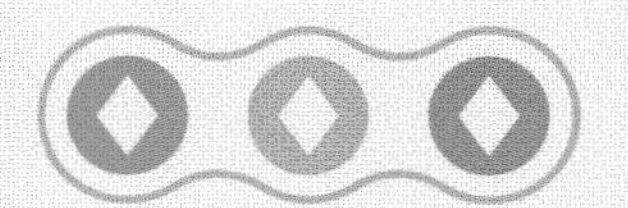

Rose and Hope hop to the stove. Near the stove, they get the note.

Skip to the spoke that broke to find the next note.

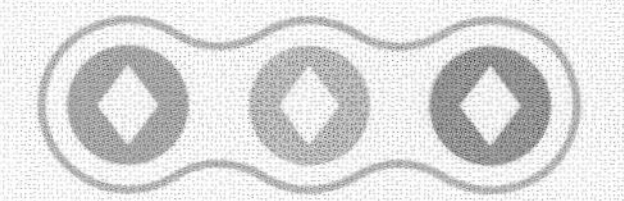

Rose and Hope see the note on the broken spoke.

Remember the mole?
Remember his hole?
Put on your coat.
Your next clue is
near the mole hole.

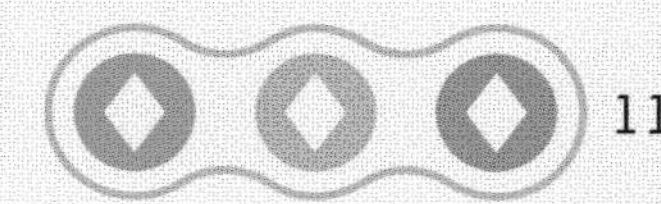

They run to the mole hole and get the note.

Slip, slip, slide
to the carrot nose
that froze.

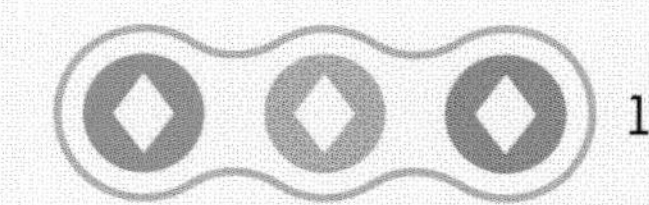

Rose and Hope slip and slide down the hill. They get the note on the snowman's nose.

Zip to the bone zone
for your next clue.

They run to the bones and look for the note.

Go to the pole.
Look in the big hole.
Inside the big hole
is your next note.

Rose and Hope race to the pole. They find the hole in the pole and a note.

Jog to the rope on a slope. You're getting close!

They tug on the rope
and get the note.

Jog to the old stone home. Go inside. You will get a birthday surprise!

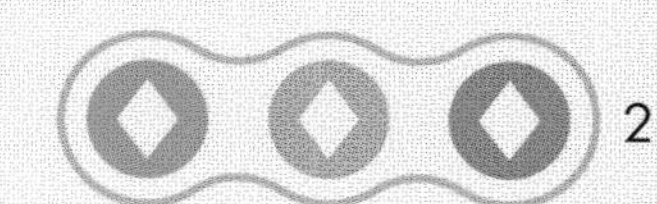

Rose and Hope jog to the stone home. They call, "Mom?!" "Dad?!"

"Happy birthday,
Rose and Hope!"

"What a surprise!"

Activities

hole
bone
nose
stone

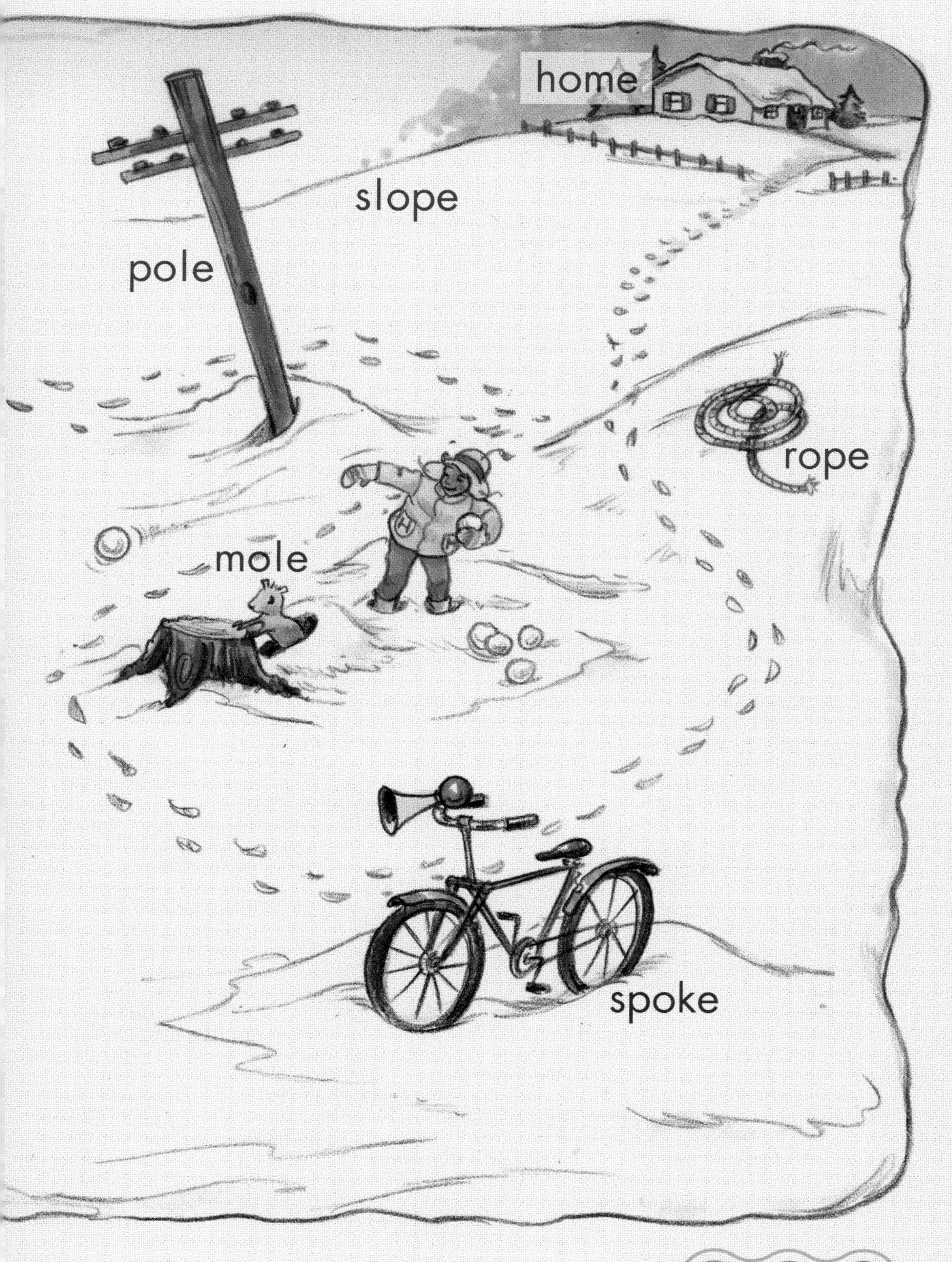
home
slope
pole
rope
mole
spoke

Rose and Hope's Birthday Surprise!

1. woke up

4. cone

5. mole hole

8. stone home

2. robes

3. note

6. pole

7. rope on a slope

Words You're Learning

Long Vowel: o_e

Skill Words

bone	froze	nose	rope	stone
broke	hole	note	Rose	stove
close	Hope	pole	slope	woke
cloves	lone	robes	spoke	zone
cone	mole			

Sight Words

call	put	your
have	that	

Challenging Words

are	dear	near	they
begin	down	next	twins
birthday	find	remember	under
broken	getting	snowman's	we'll
carrot	happy	surprise	you're
clue	inside	there	